WHO WERE THEY REALLY?

THE TRUE STORIES BEHIND FAMOUS CHARACTERS

Susan Beth Pfeffer

THE MILLBROOK PRESS
BROOKFIELD, CONNECTICUT

Published by The Millbrook Press, Inc.
2 Old New Milford Road
Brookfield, CT   06804
Visit us at our Web site: http://www.millbrookpress.com

Library of Congress Cataloging-in-Publication Data
Pfeffer, Susan Beth, 1948–
Who were they really? : the true stories behind
famous characters / Susan Beth Pfeffer.
p. cm.
Contents: Alice in Wonderland—Peter Pan—Little women—The
little mermaid—Mother Goose—Jane Eyre—Betsy Tacy—Misty of
Chincoteague—Christopher Robin—Winnie the Pooh—Peter
Rabbit—Paddington Bear—Laura Ingalls Wilder.
ISBN 0-7613-0405-3 (lib. bdg.)
1. Children's stories, English—History and criticism—Juvenile
literature. 2. Children's stories, American—History and criticism—
Juvenile literature. 3. Characters and characteristics in literature—
Juvenile literature. [1. Characters in literature.] I. Title.
PR830.C513P44 1999
820.9'9287—dc21   98-47826 CIP AC

CONTENTS

FOREWORD

"Where do you get your ideas?"

That's the question writers hear most often, and the question that's hardest to answer. Many times writers don't know where their ideas spring from. They just show up one day in their imagination, demanding to be developed and turned into a story or novel.

Sometimes a character comes first in the writer's imagination. And sometimes the character is a real person.

Who Were They Really? is about real people who were turned into famous story characters. One of them was a young woman whose refusal to marry the man who loved her inspired him to turn her into an unfeeling fairy-tale prince. A great queen of England is known to centuries of children as the cat with a fiddle (and her boyfriend as a laughing little dog). The son of a writer must live with the burden of having his name known to children throughout the world.

Other people led more ordinary lives before evolving into much-loved characters. Four sisters growing up before the Civil War become four sisters growing up during the Civil War. Five brothers immortalized as the Little Lost Boys do, in some ways, become lost when both their parents die. Two mothers write down near-accurate versions of their midwestern childhoods for their daughters, and create characters known throughout America as a result. Even pets and toys are not immune from the fictional powers of a writer.

The cliché goes that truth is stranger than fiction. On occasion it's also wilder, scarier, and sadder. No one lives planning to become a fictional character, but writers take their inspiration from everywhere, including the people they know and the places in which they have lived. Through the writers' genius, these characters live on well past the lives of their inspirations.

ALICE IN WONDERLAND

The Reverend Charles Lutwidge Dodgson was a most unusual man. At the age of nineteen he became a student at Christ Church College (part of Oxford University in England). He spent the rest of his life there, first as a student and then as a professor of mathematics. He also liked to draw, but when his pictures were rejected by a magazine, he turned to the new art of photography. Under the name of Lewis Carroll, he wrote *Alice's Adventures in Wonderland* and *Through the Looking-Glass and What Alice Found There*, books better known to generations of children as *Alice in Wonderland*.

In 1856, Dodgson met Harry, Lorina, Edith, and Alice, the young children of Henry Liddell, the dean of Christ Church College. Dodgson liked all the children, but he felt a special fondness for little Alice, then almost four. He spent many hours with the children, taking endless photographs of them. The children liked this whimsical profes-

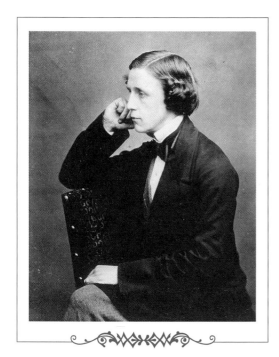

Charles took this picture of himself. He might have been trying out a new camera.

sor, and they enjoyed posing for his pictures and listening to the stories he made up for them.

One lazy summer afternoon, when Dodgson and the Liddell girls were rowing together, he made up the story of Alice and her adventures in Wonderland. When the children said good-bye that day, Alice, now ten years old, asked him to write down the story. Dodgson agreed, and spent most of that night with pen to paper.

It took him more than two years to give the manuscript to Alice. During that time, Dodgson added many new adventures to the ones he'd made up that sunny day. And although he had had no thoughts of publication when he'd first told the story to Alice and her sisters, by the time he had finished the copy for her, Dodgson had talked to a publisher about the story and found John Tenniel to draw the now-famous illustrations.

There were details in the stories that Alice Liddell must have recognized from her life. She and her sisters frequently went rowing

Above: *From the left are Alice, Lorina, Harry, and Edith in about 1859. In those days, people had to be perfectly still for forty-two seconds so the photograph did not blur. You can imagine how hard that is to do when you are just a little kid. Try it.*
Right: *When Charles took pictures of Alice, her mother liked her to be properly dressed. This is Alice's very proper purse. It is white leather, lined with rose-pink satin.*

with Dodgson. They played croquet together. Alice and her sisters had pet kittens. Two royal events, the wedding of the Prince of Wales and then a visit by the Prince and Princess of Wales to Oxford, also found their ways into the stories, which are filled with royal characters. But Alice must surely have enjoyed most the portrayal of her governess, Miss Prickett, as the prickly Red Queen.

By the time *Alice's Adventures in Wonderland* was published, Dodgson was no longer allowed to visit with his young friends. It is believed by many that Mrs. Liddell was worried about Dodgson caring too deeply for Alice. Mrs. Liddell was ambitious for her daughters and wanted them to marry men of wealth and position.

When Alice was twenty, Queen Victoria's youngest son, Prince Leopold, came to study at Christ Church College, and he and Alice fell in love. This match would have suited Mrs. Liddell perfectly, but Queen Victoria wasn't about to let her son marry a commoner. He later married Princess Helen Frederica Augusta of Waldeck-Pyrmont.

Alice finally married at the age of twenty-eight. Her husband was Reginald Hargreaves, a wealthy young man. They had three sons, Alan, Leopold, and Caryl, and lived on Hargreaves's estates. She knew great sorrow as her two older sons died in World War I, and then her

Sir John Tenniel was the artist chosen to illustrate the Alice books. This is one of his sketches. When the time came to illustrate the second Alice book Sir John wanted no part of it, as Charles was so difficult to work with. Aren't we lucky that Charles was able to change Sir John's mind?

husband died, leaving her without enough money for the kind of life she was used to.

Alice auctioned off the handwritten copy of *Alice's Adventures in Wonderland* (which is now kept at the British Museum). She got fifteen thousand pounds, which was a fortune in those days, but even that money didn't last.

Alice, when she was on her New York trip in 1932

In 1932, on the hundredth anniversary of Charles Dodgson's birth, Alice was invited to the United States for the celebration. She was eighty years old then, and enjoyed the fuss everyone made over her. She was given an honorary degree from Columbia University, spoke on the radio, and was interviewed for the *New York Times*.

After her return to England, she began to turn down other such invitations. She admitted to her son that she was "tired of being Alice in Wonderland. Does it sound ungrateful? It *is*—only I do get tired!"

Alice Liddell Hargreaves died in 1934, at the age of eighty-two. She may have been tired of being Alice in Wonderland, but the world has never tired of the character she inspired.

PETER PAN

Have you ever wanted not to grow up, but to stay a child forever? That was the dream of Peter Pan, who lived in Never-Never Land with the Lost Boys and fought the terrible pirate, Captain Hook.

The boys who inspired the creation of Peter Pan and his friends seemed to have lives as enchanted as Peter Pan's. There were five brothers in all, George, John, Peter, Michael, and Nicholas Llewelyn Davies. Their father was Arthur Llewelyn Davies, a lawyer. Their mother, Sylvia, was the sister of a well-known actor named Gerald du Maurier. Arthur and Sylvia loved each other and their sons very much. They were an extremely appealing family. So it was no surprise that Sir James M. Barrie, a well-known playwright, grew close to them and to their five young sons.

Barrie and the Llewelyn Davies family spent summers together, with Barrie inventing games for the boys to play. A calm English lake became a South Seas lagoon. Peaceful forests became tropical forests, filled with dangerous enemies. The older boys were transformed into pirates. And when the transformation was complete, Barrie wrote the play *Peter Pan*.

Pirates, all. Here are George, Jack, and Peter in the middle of a battle.

Peter Pan was an enormous hit when it first opened in London. Captain Hook, that terrible villain, was acted by the Llewelyn Davies boys' uncle, Gerald du Maurier. The boys knew they had inspired the play, and that only made them feel closer to Barrie.

Their own childhood wasn't to last forever, the way Peter Pan's did. Shortly after *Peter Pan* opened, Arthur Llewelyn Davies developed cancer. He died in 1907, leaving a young widow and five sons, the oldest of whom was fourteen, and the youngest just three. Over the next few years Sylvia Llewelyn Davies turned more and more to Barrie for emotional and financial help. Barrie helped pay for the boys' education and spent as much time with them as he could.

Then, only three years later, Sylvia Llewelyn Davies died, also of cancer. Now the five boys were orphans.

Michael and Sir James M. Barrie. Michael inspired lots of scenes that found their way into Peter Pan. Once during a night walk through the woods Michael saw a twinkle of light, which inspired the character of Tinkerbell.

Sir James and his dog Luath, who inspired Nana, perhaps because of the gentle manner Luath took with the boys.

James M. Barrie became their unofficial guardian. He continued to pay for their education and helped them with their careers. But he didn't just throw money at them. He wrote to Michael and Nicholas, the two youngest boys, every day when they were away at school, and all the boys spent their vacations with him. Although they had many aunts and uncles on both their father's and mother's sides, it was "Uncle Jim" who raised them and called them "my boys."

The suffering of the boys had not yet ended. George, the oldest, was killed in World War I. And Michael, who was Barrie's favorite, drowned, along with a friend, while a student at Oxford.

Unlike Peter Pan, John, Peter, and Nicholas Llewelyn Davies grew up, worked at jobs, married, and had children. James M. Barrie remained a part of their lives, and Peter and Nicholas were at his bedside when he died.

LITTLE WOMEN

Write about what you know best. This advice has been given to young authors for many years now. But few have made better use of that advice than Louisa May Alcott.

Louisa was the second of four daughters born to Bronson Alcott, a teacher and philosopher, and Abigail (Abba) May Alcott, called Marmee by her daughters. Louisa May Alcott's oldest sister, Anna, loved her home and family. Lizzie, who was next in age to Louisa, was a quiet girl who died young. And May, the youngest, was an artist.

In *Little Women*, Louisa May Alcott transformed Bronson and Abba Alcott to Father and Marmee March, turned Anna into Meg, who loved her home and family, Lizzie into Beth, who was quiet and died young, and May into Amy, an artist. She hardly even changed their names. And of course, Louisa May Alcott, the writer, became Jo March, whose dream it was to be a writer.

*Louisa May Alcott,
whose love and
respect for her mother
helped her create one
of the most well-loved
characters in
American literature,
Marmee March.*

Abba Alcott in Bronson Alcott's study. Abba probably only sat long enough for this photograph to be taken. As the wife of a philosopher who spent much of his time thinking big, deep thoughts, Abba had much work to do to keep food on the table for her family.

Of course there were differences between the Alcotts and the Marches. Bronson Alcott was seemingly incapable of holding a job, and was frequently bailed out of financial disaster by his friends and Abba's family. Abba was more than just a loving mother. Among other things, she worked as a social worker in Boston. And her marriage wasn't always a happy one.

When *Little Women* begins, Father March is a chaplain in the Civil War. In reality, it was Louisa May Alcott who participated in the war, working as a nurse in Washington, D.C., for three weeks, until serious illness forced Bronson to bring her home.

Although Anna and May married, just as Meg and Amy did, their husbands were quite different from the ones Louisa created for them. They both married men much younger than they were (in May's case, she was thirty-seven and he twenty-two). And unlike Jo, Louisa May

This schedule for Louisa May and her sisters was probably Bronson's idea, no doubt arrived at after a great deal of thought and consideration.

Order of In-door Duties
for Children.

Hillside 1846

Morning		Fore noon		Noon	Afternoon		Evening
5	Rise, Bathe, Dress	9	Studies with Mr Lane.		1	Rest	6. Supper, Recreation, Conversation, Music
6	Breakfast	10½	Recreations.	12 Dinner.	2	Sewing, Conversation, and Reading, with Mother and Miss Ford	
.	Housewifery	11	Studies with Father		4	Errands and (Leaves) Recreations.	8.
.	Recreations. (Leaves in care of Miss Ford)						8½ Bed

Vigilance, Punctuality, Perseverance.
Prompt, Cheerful, Unquestioning, Obedience.
Government of Temper, Hands, and Tongue.
Gentle Manners, Motions, and Words.
Work, Studies, and Play distinct.
No interchange of Labors.

Bathing Hours
5._ 10¾ 5..

Study Hours
9 & 10½. 11 & 12.

Labor Hours
6¾ & 8. 2 & 4.

Play Hours
8 to 9. 10 & 10½. 4 to 6.

Eating Hours
6 & 6½. 12 & 12½. 6 & 6½.

Sleeping Hours
8 to 5. 8½ to 5

Observe Silence and Stillness.

The Alcotts in front of their home, Orchard House. On Monday nights the Alcotts entertained their neighbors with plays performed by the girls, philosophical discussions with Bronson, and goodies from Abba's kitchen.

Alcott remained single. She would have been just as happy to keep Jo single as well, but her readers wanted Jo to marry.

Two years after May was married, she gave birth to a daughter, whom she named for her sister Louisa. May died in childbirth, and the baby, known as Lulu, was brought to Louisa and her father to be raised.

On March 4, 1888, Bronson Alcott died at the age of eighty-eight. Two days later, Louisa also died, her body worn out by a variety of ailments. She was fifty-six. Only her oldest sister, Anna, survived her. Their niece, Lulu, went to Europe to live with her father.

Write about what you know. Louisa certainly did that when she wrote of the family theatrics, her beloved sister's death, Jo's literary ambitions and Amy's artistic ones, and Meg's happy home. Marmee, the adored mother, was true to Louisa's vision of her (although, in Louisa's own words, "not half good enough"). Not all the characters, however, sprang from Louisa's childhood memories. Laurie, the boy next door, was based on a young man Louisa met in 1865, and the much-dreaded Aunt March was created entirely by Louisa.

Louisa May Alcott, abolitionist, suffragette, independent woman, led a life far more complicated and probably not as happy as Jo March's. But in Jo, her sisters, and their parents, she created a loving family that has lived on far longer than she could have ever dreamed.

THE LITTLE MERMAID

Once upon a time, a young man named Hans Christian Andersen was in love.

He had never been in love before. His life had been filled with twists and turns. His father died when Hans was eleven, and it had been a struggle for the boy to get an education.

But theater was his true love, and Hans sang for a living until his voice changed. His dreams turned to writing, and he was supported in his dream by many of the people he met in his native Denmark.

Hans's chief sponsor was a man named Jonas Collin. Collin had many children, and Hans loved spending time with the family.

When he was twenty-five years old, Hans fell in love. The woman was Riborg Voigt, the younger sister of one of Hans's friends. Love

Hans Christian Andersen, whose unrequited loves inspired him to write many heart-breaking stories.

was such an unusual sensation for Hans that he didn't even realize that was what was making him obsess over this young woman until friends teased him about being in love.

But once Hans Christian Andersen knew he was in love, he accepted the depths of his feelings for Riborg. The only problem was, Riborg was unofficially engaged to another.

Andersen wrote her a letter, filled with his yearning for her. He begged her to be sure she truly loved her fiancé. If she didn't, then Andersen would work to prove himself worthy of her.

Alas, Riborg was in love with her fiancé, and she wrote to Andersen to tell him so. The next time she saw Andersen, she whispered, "Farewell forever," to him.

Andersen was devastated and wrote to a friend that he wished he were dead. But life went on, and Andersen traveled to Germany, where he read the fairy tales of the Brothers Grimm.

When Andersen returned to Denmark, he resumed his friendship with the Collin family. He began to tell his sad story of unrequited love to Louise Collin, aged eighteen. Louise was more than willing to listen to Hans, whom she had known since she was a little girl and he had cut out paper dolls for her.

Before he knew it, Hans Christian Andersen was in love again.

Riborg Voigt may have been wonderful, but Hans also lived during a time when romance and things romantic were very important. It may have been the times he lived in, as much as anything else, that caused Hans to behave so dramatically about losing Riborg. Of course, she may truly have been the love of his life. Upon his death a leather necklace found around his neck contained the farewell letter she wrote to him so many years before.

One time Hans went to visit the family of Charles Dickens, another great writer. Dickens's son wrote that while Hans himself was somewhat odd, his beautiful paper cutouts of "fairies and animals of all kinds . . . might well have stepped out of the pages of his books."

But once again, Andersen had picked a woman whose heart was elsewhere. Louise was in love with a young lawyer, and her engagement was announced a few months later.

For the second time, Andersen was heartbroken. Four years later, he used some of his feelings for Louise by turning her into the character of the prince in his classic fairy tale "The Little Mermaid."

The statue of the Little Mermaid in Copenhagen. Visitors touch it for good luck.

Usually a prince in a fairy tale is a heroic figure, a handsome young man who proves his worthiness by rescuing the princess. But in "The Little Mermaid," it's the mermaid who rescues the prince, and the prince is so unaware, he doesn't even realize it's the mermaid who has saved his life. He falls in love with another and forces the mermaid to choose between her own life and his. Her great love for him allows her to sacrifice her life that he might live with the woman he loves. And throughout it all, he thinks of the little mermaid as nothing more than a charming pet.

"The Little Mermaid" was one of Andersen's favorite stories, and it was clear that he identified with the mermaid, who loved purely and in vain. The Danes loved "The Little Mermaid" as much as its creator did. It was turned into a ballet, danced by Jonas Collin's great-granddaughter. Her performance inspired a wealthy gentleman to commission a statue of the Little Mermaid, which to this day remains a much-loved Danish landmark.

That's as close to a fairy tale ending as Hans Christian Andersen could have dreamed of.

MOTHER GOOSE

"There was an old lady who lived in a shoe
She had so many children she didn't know what to do."

For centuries, children have been entertained, or put to sleep, by the rhymes and lullabies that are lumped under the category of "Mother Goose Rhymes." But was there a real Mother Goose, and what are the origins of some of the more famous songs?

Indeed, there could have been a Mother Goose. In fact, there may have been several Mother Gooses.

According to some scholars, Mother Goose was actually the Queen of Sheba, famed in the Bible. Others believe her to have been Queen Bertha of France, the mother of Charlemagne.

Old Mother Goose, when
She wanted to wander,
Would ride through the air
On a very fine gander.

Is this the Mother Goose you remember from your childhood days? Many different artists have drawn Mother Goose over the years.

Queen Bertha, who died in 783, was known as Queen Goose-foot, or Goose-footed Bertha, because her feet reminded her subjects of a goose.

Goose-footed Bertha is portrayed in French legends as working at a spinning wheel, while children surround her listening to her stories. In France, Mother Goose was known for her stories rather than her rhymes. Charles Perrault, in 1697, published a volume of fairy tales (including "Cinderella" and "Sleeping Beauty") as *Tales of My Mother Goose*. In England, as well, Mother Goose was identified as a storyteller.

The United States has its own candidate for Mother Goose. In 1692, Elizabeth Foster married a man named Isaac Goose. Elizabeth immediately became a mother of a large brood of children, since Mr. Goose, a widower, already had ten children. Mr. and Mrs. Goose then had another six children together.

Years later, a son-in-law named Thomas Fleet published the rhymes he had heard Elizabeth recite to entertain her grandchildren. The book was called *Mother Goose's Melodies*, but no copies exist today, and there is no proof that Mrs. Goose was Mother Goose.

However, it is certain is that many of the Mother Goose rhymes go back centuries before Elizabeth Foster ever met Isaac Goose. In fact, choosing rhymes such as "Eenie Meenie Minee Mo" are believed to be versions of rhymes that the Druids, who lived in England over two thousand years ago, used to select human sacrifices.

Just as no one can be certain who Mother Goose really was, no one can say for sure how the different rhymes came into being. Take, for example:

> *Jack and Jill went up a hill*
> *To fetch a pail of water.*
> *Jack fell down and broke his crown*
> *And Jill came tumbling after.*

According to the Reverend Sabine Baring-Gould (1834–1924), an Icelandic scholar (better known as the author of the hymn "Onward, Christian Soldiers"), Jack and Jill are actually Hjuki and Bil, two Norse names. Hjuki is pronounced Juki, and over the centuries Bil turned into Jill.

But Katherine Elwes Thomas, who believed many of the Mother Goose rhymes were written during the reigns of Henry VIII and Queen Elizabeth I, was sure that the hill Jack and Jill went up was actually a reference to a trip made to France to arrange for a marriage between a French prince and Henry VIII's oldest daughter, Mary.

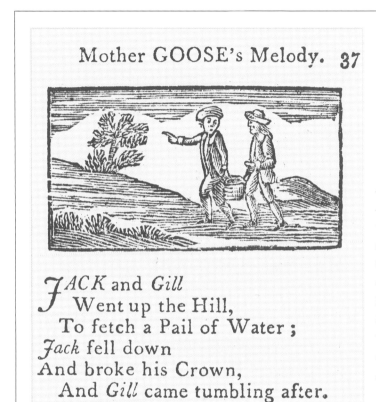

JACK and *Gill*
  Went up the Hill,
   To fetch a Pail of Water;
Jack fell down
And broke his Crown,
  And *Gill* came tumbling after.

In this edition of Mother Goose, Jill is Gill, a boy. While some of the rhymes changed through history, the interesting thing is how many of them were repeated word for word, staying exactly the same for hundreds of years.

And still another scholar, Lewis Spence, in 1947, pointed out that no one goes up a hill to fetch water unless that water is very special indeed, and claimed the rhyme referred to a mystic ritual that would have dated well before Princess Mary needed a husband.

Another Mother Goose rhyme that seemingly makes no sense at all has inspired many different explanations.

Hey diddle, diddle,
The cat and the fiddle,
The cow jumped over the moon.
The little dog laughed
To see such sport,
And the dish ran away with the spoon.

It is believed by many that this nonsense verse refers to several different people in the reign of Elizabeth I, starting with that great queen herself. Her nickname was "the Cat" because of the way she played with politicians in her court. And she was known for her love of fiddle music. The little dog might be a reference to a man named Robert Dudley, who Queen Elizabeth thought about marrying (and about whom she once said, "He is like my little lap-dog," which is the sort of thing a queen can say about a boyfriend).

Even the dish and spoon can be traced to a real life Elizabethan couple. "The dish" was the title of a nobleman whose job it was to carry golden dishes into the state dining room. And "the spoon" was a beautiful young woman who tasted the food before the queen did, just in case someone had slipped a little poison into it.

One such dish-and-spoon couple were the Earl of Hertford and Lady Katherine Grey, who fell in love and were secretly married. When Queen Elizabeth found out, she had them imprisoned in the Tower of London, where they lived for seven years and had two children.

Now that you see the Dish and the Spoon, and know a little about Queen Elizabeth, does the nursery rhyme seem different to you?

Throughout the centuries, countless children have been lulled to sleep by the gentle song "Rockabye Baby, on the tree top." Again, there are many theories about the origin of this lullaby. Katherine Elwes Thomas believed the song was political and referred to James Stuart, pretender to the English throne (whose dreams of ruling Great Britain crashed as certainly as the cradle in the lullaby).

But there's another American legend about "Rockabye Baby." According to that legend, the song was written by a young person who came over on the *Mayflower* and saw Indian mothers rocking their children in birchbark cradles in the boughs of trees.

And finally, what of that old woman who lived in the shoe? It's tempting to think she refers to the American Mother Goose, with all her stepchildren, children, and grandchildren. But, alas, she was not its inspiration. The rhyme predates her, and is believed by many scholars to have nothing to do with real mothers and children, or even shoes. Instead, they think it refers to the government of Great Britain, which lived in a shoe (the British Isles) and had so many "children," meaning colonies all over the world. One of those colonies, of course, became the United States of America, just a few decades after Elizabeth Foster became Mother Goose.

BETSY-TACY

"What was it like when you were my age?"

Have you ever asked your parents that question, and have they ever responded with stories about their friendships, the games they played, the schools they went to, and the fights they had with their brothers and sisters? And has it seemed almost unbelievable to you that your parents ever could have been kids just like you?

Merian Lovelace was a little girl in the 1930s when she asked her mother, Maud Hart Lovelace, to tell her stories of her childhood at the beginning of the twentieth century. And Maud Hart Lovelace told story after story about herself and her best friend, Frances Kenney. In fact, Merian Lovelace enjoyed hearing the stories so much that Maud Hart Lovelace decided to put them down on paper. And thus was born the Betsy-Tacy series of books.

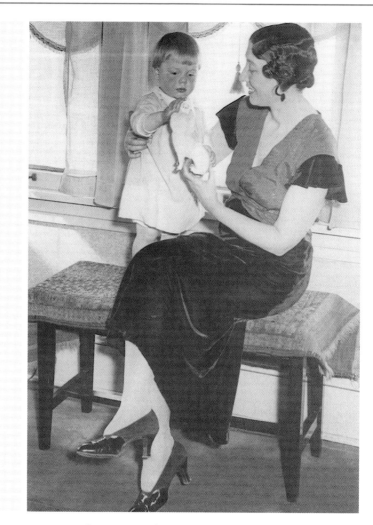

Maud Hart Lovelace with her daughter Merian.

Mrs. Lovelace had grown up in a small Minnesota town named Mankato, but in the stories she changed the names of the people and places. The town was renamed Deep Valley. She herself became Betsy Ray, and Frances turned into Tacy. Mrs. Lovelace gave her sisters different names as well, but she kept many of the details of their lives, including the fact that her father owned a shoe store and that her family lived in a small yellow house.

Maud and her little sister in the front hall of their little yellow house. They are on their way to school.

Maud and her best friend Frances dressed up for Halloween. They had so many real-life adventures it must not have been too difficult for Maud to find something new and exciting to share in the many books she wrote.

The characters in the *Betsy-Tacy* stories grow up, and for Mrs. Lovelace it was no problem to decide how they would behave as they grew older. She had kept diaries throughout her years in high school, and used the material she had recorded to make sure Betsy's and Tacy's feelings and activities remained true to life.

In 1961 the mayor of Mankato declared a Betsy-Tacy Day, and many of the real people who inspired characters in the books returned for the celebration.

A famous illustrator named Lois Lenski illustrated nearly all of the Betsy-Tacy books, and the characters she drew are how most people envision Betsy and Tacy.

And what of Merian Lovelace? She went to Smith College, where she let her friends read the unpublished chapters of the latest *Betsy-Tacy* stories. She became a writer, too, although a different sort than her mother. Her father was a journalist, and that's what Merian Lovelace became.

But she remained a true Betsy-Tacy fan for the rest of her life, working with the Betsy-Tacy Society and seeing to it that her mother's books remained in print so that new generations of children could enjoy the same stories that her mother had told to her.

MISTY OF CHINCOTEAGUE

Some people love animals. Some people love writing. And some lucky people love both.

When Marguerite Breithaupt was a little girl growing up in Milwaukee, her father owned a printing shop, and he would let his daughter read the proofs he printed. When she was ten, she decided to become a writer, which she promptly did. The next year a national women's magazine published one of her works, and she was on her way.

It wasn't until after she married Sidney Crocker Henry and moved with him to a farm in Wayne, Illinois, that Marguerite Henry became interested in writing about animals. But once she did, she discovered her true gift.

Misty of Chincoteague is her most famous book, and one of the most beloved horse books of all time. Marguerite Henry went to the

The day Marguerite had been waiting for: Misty has arrived to live with the Henrys. Marguerite thought that having Misty playing in the paddock outside as she wrote would help her bring Misty's character alive on paper. It worked!

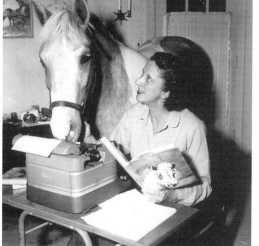

Marguerite Henry and her beloved Misty at the typewriter. It looks like Misty wants to see what happens next!

island of Chincoteague in Virginia to research the rounding up of the wild horses on the nearby island of Assateague. Every year the people of Chincoteague have a Pony Penning Day, when the wild horses are sold. It was at a Pony Penning Day that Marguerite Henry saw the foal that she named Misty.

Some credit for the popularity of Marguerite's three Chincoteague stories has to go to the illustrator, Wesley Dennis. Marguerite invited Wesley along on her first trip to Chincoteague and together they worked on Misty, Sea Star *and* Stormy, *as well as many other books. Sometimes it takes the right pairing of an author and an illustrator to bring out the genius of each. Marguerite Henry and Wesley Dennis were quite a team.*

Marguerite Henry wasn't satisfied with simply seeing a young pony and creating a character for it. She brought Misty back to Illinois with her, and the pony lived on the Henry farm for several years.

Marguerite Henry grew quite famous from *Misty of Chincoteague*, and so did Misty. The pony was invited to a conference of the American Library Association and had a movie made about her life. When Misty went from Illinois back to Chincoteague, it was a news event, with reporters from all over the United States there to cover it. And when Misty's first colt needed a name, schoolchildren by the thousands wrote in with their suggestions (Mrs. Henry decided to go with "Stormy").

Marguerite Henry lived to be nintey-five years old. But thanks to her love of animals and her love of writing, Misty the pony from Chincoteague will live forever.

CHRISTOPHER ROBIN

Little boys from wealthy families in England in the 1920s all led similar lives. They were brought up by nannies and had very limited contact with their parents. They were given toys and pets (usually dogs), taught their prayers, instructed in manners and games, and when they were eight or nine, sent to boarding schools.

In many ways, Christopher Robin Milne's childhood was typical of a wealthy little English boy. But there was one huge difference. His childhood, even as he lived it, was being immortalized by his father, A. A. Milne, in two volumes of verse, *When We Were Very Young* and *Now We Are Six,* and two volumes of stories, *Winnie the Pooh* and *The House at Pooh Corner*. When people met Christopher Robin Milne, they knew all about him and his much-loved teddy bear. His very name proclaimed whom he was to everyone he met.

This is a famous photograph of A.A. Milne and his son, Christopher Robin, who is holding Winnie-the-Pooh.

Perhaps A. A. Milne didn't worry about using Christopher Robin's name because he never called him that. To his father, young Christopher was Billy Moon, or more frequently, just Moon. But Moon was a private nickname, not even used by Christopher's mother, and when the boy went to school, he was known by the name his father had made so famous.

There were other ways that Christopher Milne's childhood was different. For one thing, he was an only child whose mother had very much wanted a daughter. It's possible this is why Christopher's hair was kept much longer than was the fashion for little boys, and he was dressed in an unusual, almost girl-like, fashion. The illustrator of the Winnie the Pooh books, Ernest H. Shepard, portrayed Christopher just as he was, with the long hair and the girl-like clothing. That didn't help the shy boy make friends when at the age of nine he was sent away to boarding school.

Mr. Milne gave this picture of Christopher to the illustrator E. H. Shepard and, as you can see, Mr. Shepard found it very helpful from haircut to shoes. This picture appears in The House at Pooh Corner.

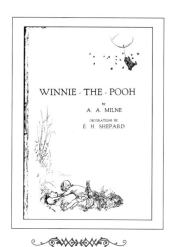

But it wasn't all bad being Christopher Robin Milne. He received fan mail from all over the world, and he enjoyed being a bit of a celebrity. He even got to walk in a parade, carrying his famous stuffed animals. And he was very close to his father. They did math problems together, and crosswords, looked for birds' nests at their country home, and played cricket and golf. By spending so much time with his son, A. A. Milne developed a real understanding of the way little boys speak and feel.

Christopher Milne fought in World War II and was injured. Following the war, he returned home and married a cousin from his mother's side of the family. He and his wife opened a bookstore, and that was how they supported themselves and their daughter for many years. Christopher Milne was very proud of the fact that even though it was his childhood and his toys that inspired his father to write the classic children's stories, he never used any of the money from *Winnie the Pooh* to support himself financially.

WINNIE THE POOH

When Christopher Robin Milne was one year old, he was given a teddy bear, soon known to the world as Winnie the Pooh. Shortly after that, he was given a toy donkey named Eeyore. A neighbor gave Christopher Piglet, and these three toys inspired A. A. Milne to write his stories.

Milne needed more characters, so he created Owl and Rabbit. Later, he and his wife bought Christopher a stuffed kangaroo named Kanga and a tiger named Tigger. Kanga (and her baby, Roo) and Tigger were selected both to make Christopher happy and to provide Milne with story possibilities.

Christopher played with Pooh, and his mother played with him. Christopher's father started listening in and took the character of his son and his toys and used them for his books. Illustrator Ernest

Christopher Robin's Pooh, Kanga, Piglet, Eeyore, and Tigger.
They live at the Donnell Library in New York City. In 1998 a
member of the British Parliament suggested that perhaps Pooh
and his friends should be brought home to England, but the
mayor of New York City replied that he had spoken to Pooh, who
was very happy indeed right where he was.

Shepard drew Christopher Robin and Pooh and the places they played, and when the books came out, readers knew just what the boy and his toys looked like.

When Christopher went to school, he was too old to play with stuffed animals, no matter how famous they might be. By that time, Roo had been lost in the woods somewhere. To protect the remaining world-famous toys, battered, sewn up, bitten, and much loved, a glass case was built for them in the Milne family house.

In 1947, A. A. Milne's publisher, Elliott Macrae, came to visit and saw Pooh and his friends. Milne gave Macrae the toys, and with Milne's permission, Pooh, Eeyore, and the rest went on a promotional tour of the United States. Later, Macrae kept the toys on display in the office of his publishing house, E. P. Dutton.

In 1987, Elliott Macrae donated Pooh, Piglet, Eeyore, Kanga, and Tigger to the New York City Public Library. They are visited annually by three-quarters of a million people, who marvel at how small Piglet is (four and a half inches) and how Eeyore's tail is pinned on, and what a sweet smile Kanga has, and how well-loved and well-worn Winnie the Pooh is. For a bear of very little brain, it is quite nice to be fussed over by many people.

PETER RABBIT

Beatrix Potter was the oldest child and only daughter of Rupert and Helen Potter. She and her younger brother, Bertram, were brought up by nannies and governesses. It was a comfortable life, made even better by long summer holidays in the country.

Beatrix's father was a lawyer, but he had an artistic side. He sketched pictures and took lots of photographs of his family and friends. Beatrix loved to draw as well, and never really wanted to do anything else with her life. Since her family had money, there was no need for her to get a job.

She and Bertram loved animals and always had an assortment of rabbits, ducks, even bats, in their home. Beatrix drew the animals. She wasn't skillful at drawing people, and had little actual art training, but she was gifted at capturing animals on paper.

Beatrix's father was an amateur photographer who took many pictures of his family over the years. Here is a photograph of Beatrix and Spot, the family dog, taken when Beatrix was about seventeen. Beatrix loved Spot, and obviously Spot loved Beatrix. Look how happy he is to relax on her lap.

Beatrix with her rabbit Benjamin Bouncer.

At the age of twenty-four, Beatrix acquired a rabbit as a pet and named him Benjamin Bouncer. She drew pictures of Benjamin and sold them as Christmas and New Year's cards. And that was how she became a professional artist.

In 1893, when Beatrix was twenty-seven, she bought another rabbit as a pet and named it Peter Piper. Peter went everywhere with her and was her beloved pet for nine years. He was, as Beatrix put it, "an affectionate companion and quiet friend."

But Peter was more than that. He was also an inspiration to Beatrix. One of her friends was Annie Moore, who had been her governess when Beatrix was sixteen. Annie Moore was married and had several children, whom Beatrix was fond of visiting. One day, soon after the arrival of Peter, Beatrix wrote a letter about Peter to Annie's son Noel. And that was how Peter Rabbit was created.

Beatrix Potter continued to use real animals as the basis for her drawings. For *The Tale of Squirrel Nutkin*, she bought two squirrels from a pet shop. The squirrels didn't like each other and fought all the time. Beatrix was forced to get rid of the better looking of the squirrels and was stuck with "a nice little animal, but half of one ear has been bitten off, which spoils his appearance!"

Beatrix's menagerie grew. She acquired a hedgehog, which she named Mrs. Tiggy-winkle ("a dear person; just like a very fat, rather stupid little dog"). Her two pet mice, Tom Thumb and Hunca Munca, were later the models for *The Tale of Two Bad Mice*. A duck on her farm became Jemima Puddle-Duck. Even rats brought out the artist

Eastwood Dunkeld
Sep 4th 93

My dear Noel,
I don't know what to write to you, so I shall tell you a story about four little rabbits whose names were—

Flopsy, Mopsy, Cottontail and Peter

They lived with their mother in a sand bank under the root of a big fir tree.

Annie's son Noel was sick and had to stay in bed. This letter to Noel, which ended up being The Tale of Peter Rabbit, was started as a way to cheer up a sick friend.

and animal lover in Beatrix. She used one as inspiration for Samuel Whiskers.

Beatrix Potter's love of animals has inspired many others, even since her death. In 1985 the Wildlife Hospitals Trust in England opened the St Tiggywinkle's Hedgehog Unit at their animal hospital. It cares for sick and injured wild birds and animals, particularly hedgehogs, hurt in accidents.

Not many hedgehogs get to have hospitals named for them. But Mrs. Tiggy-winkle was, after all, "a dear person," and she was loved by a dear person as well.

Mrs. Tiggy-winkle accompanied Beatrix on a vacation to the sea. In a letter to a friend, Beatrix wrote that Mrs. Tiggy-winkle was not fond of shrimp, and drank her milk out of a doll's teacup.

PADDINGTON BEAR

It isn't just little children who love teddy bears. Adults love them, too.

One day shortly before Christmas, television cameraman and writer Michael Bond saw a forlorn teddy bear sitting unsold in a toy store. Feeling sorry for the bear, Bond bought it to take home to his wife. Since Bond and his wife lived near the Paddington train station in London, the name Paddington Bear seemed perfect for a character. And thus, from a toy store in London, Paddington Bear from Darkest Peru was born.

Michael Bond and Paddington Bear.

Peggy Fortnum was the original illustrator of Paddington.

LAURA INGALLS WILDER

History is not usually about families, and it's even more rarely about young girls. But Laura Ingalls Wilder wrote about her life as a pioneer girl in the 1870s, and gave generations of children a view of American history they might not otherwise have gotten.

The *Little House* books tell the story of the Ingalls family as they move from town to town, growing up, meeting new people, suffering losses, and knowing great happiness in spite of the rugged conditions of their lives. It's history as average people lived it, and the stories are ones that all children can identify with.

Laura Ingalls Wilder was the second oldest of Charles and Caroline Ingalls's four daughters (the Ingallses also had a son who died in infancy). Her childhood was spent in Wisconsin, Missouri, Kansas, Minnesota, and Iowa, as her father sought work and her mother sought

The Ingalls family. From left to right, Ma, Carrie, Laura, Pa, Grace, and Mary.

stability. Charles Ingalls was a man who found it hard to stay in one place. It wasn't easy, before the invention of the moving van, for a family to pick up and leave one home to settle in another. By the time

Laura and Almanzo Wilder

Laura was nine years old, her family had lived in six different homes. When she was eleven, she had a paying job at a hotel, washing dishes, waiting on tables, cooking, and tending the hotel keeper's baby. It was a hard life, and it turned Laura into a strong, independent woman.

As a teenager, Laura lived in the Dakota territory, where she met and fell in love with Almanzo Wilder. After a two-year courtship, Laura, aged eighteen, married Almanzo, who was ten years older. In 1885, at the height of the Victorian era, when wives were expected to do what their husbands told them to do without question, Laura told the minister who performed the service to leave out the vow "to obey," and he did. Even at eighteen, Laura knew on what terms she intended to live.

Their marriage lasted from 1885 to Almanzo's death in 1949. In that time, the United States fought in three wars; radios, movies, and television were invented; the first atomic bomb was dropped; the stock market rose and crashed; and cars and airplanes made the world much smaller than could ever have been imagined.

Laura and Almanzo had one daughter, Rose. When Laura was in her sixties, she decided to put down her childhood memories for her daughter. And thus the Little House books were born.

Laura Ingalls Wilder, whose past will last long into the future as new generations discover the magic of the Little House books

But even memoirs can change fact into fiction. Laura changed her age by two years for *Little House in the Big Woods* and added her younger sister Carrie to the story, even though she had not yet been born. Sometimes the needs of a story outweigh the needs of factual retelling.

Laura's older sister Mary was blinded by a stroke as a girl and lived with her parents until their deaths. Her sister Carrie became a printer and later a newspaper manager. Laura's sister Grace and her husband were farmers. Laura's daughter, Rose, another strong woman, became a newspaper reporter.

And what of that eternal wanderer, Charles Ingalls? After many homes and many jobs, he and his wife settled down in DeSmet, in the Dakota territory. After all their Little Houses, they finally had a home.

FOR FURTHER READING

Now that you've learned the backgrounds of many classics, you might want to read the books themselves. Your library should have just about all the books mentioned in *Who Were They Really*. Here are some titles you can ask for.

Mother Goose has been the inspiration for many fine children's book illustrators. Four different versions, all published in the 1980s, are *Mother Goose,* illustrated by Brian Wildsmith; *Mother Goose: A Collection of Classic Nursery Rhymes,* illustrated by Michael Hague; *The Random House Book of Mother Goose,* illustrated by Arnold Lobel; and *Tomie de Paola's Mother Goose.*

Hans Christian Andersen's fairy tales can also be found in many different versions. In 1993, Charles Santore illustrated a version of *The Little Mermaid.* If you want to read more of Andersen's famous stories (including "The Emperor's New Clothes" and "The Ugly Duckling"), you could look for *Fairy Tales of Hans Christian Andersen* (1995), *Hans Christian Andersen Fairy Tales* (1992), or *Stories from Hans Christian Andersen* (1993).

There are two recent reprintings of *Peter Pan,* one illustrated by Michael Hague (1987), the other by Trina S. Hyman (1995).

Alice in Wonderland, Through the Looking Glass, Winnie the Pooh, and *The House at Pooh Corner* are easily available with their original classic illustrations.

Beatrix Potter's writings in newer editions include *The Complete Adventures of Peter Rabbit* (1982), *Hill Top Tales: Four Original Peter Rabbit Stories* (1989), *The Tale of Jemima Puddle Duck and Other Farmyard Tales* (1987), *The Tales of Mrs. Tiggy-Winkle* (1987), and *The Tale of Mr. Jeremy Fisher* (1989).

Paddington Bear's adventures can be enjoyed in *A Bear Called Paddington* (1960), *Paddington at Work* (1967), *Paddington Helps Out* (1973), and *More About Paddington* (1979).

If you're interested in horses, read *Misty of Chincoteague* or *Stormy, Misty's Foal.* There is also *Misty the Wonder Pony, by Misty Herself,* if you want to get the story straight from the horse's mouth.

Many versions exist of *Little Women.* If you want to follow the story of Jo March even further, read *Little Men* and *Jo's Boys.*

Betsy and Tacy's lives can be traced in such books as *Betsy-Tacy, Over the Big Hill, Down Town, Heaven to Betsy,* and *Betsy's Wedding.*

You can read about the Ingalls clan in *Little House in the Big Woods, Little House on the Prairie, On the Banks of Plum Creek, The Long Winter,* and *These Happy Golden Years,* among other titles.

Many of the books discussed in *Who Were They Really* have been turned into movies. Disney has made classic animated film versions of *Alice In Wonderland, Peter Pan,* and "The Little Mermaid," as well as shorter cartoon versions of stories from *Winnie the Pooh.* Paddington Bear has also starred in short films, the movie *Misty* retells the story of that horse, and there are at least two classic movie versions of *Little Women.*

Little House on the Prairie was the inspiration for a long-running TV series, and Peter Rabbit and friends live on in a British ballet.

Read the books or watch the videos, and be in on the secrets of who were they really!

SELECTED BIBLIOGRAPHY

Baring-Gould, William S. *The Annotated Mother Goose.* New York: Clarkson N. Potter, Inc., 1962.

Bedell, Madelon. *The Alcotts: Biography of a Family.* New York: Clarkson N. Potter, Inc., 1980.

Cohen, Morton N. *Lewis Carroll.* New York: Alfred A. Knopf, 1995.

Dunbar, Janet. *J. M. Barrie.* Boston: Houghton Mifflin Company, 1970.

Fisher, Margery. *Who's Who in Children's Books.* Austin, TX: Holt, Rinehart and Winston, 1975.

Milne, Christopher. *The Enchanted Places.* New York: E. P. Dutton & Co., Inc., 1975.

Milne, Christopher. *The Path Through the Trees.* New York: E. P. Dutton & Co., Inc., 1979.

Stirling, Monica. *The Wild Swan: The Life and Times of Hans Christian Andersen.* Orlando, FL: Harcourt, Brace & World, 1965.

Taylor, Judy. *Beatrix Potter.* New York: Frederick Warne, 1986.

Zochert, David. *Laura.* Chicago: Contemporary Books, Inc., 1976.

Something About the Author. Detroit: Gale Research Company: Volume 2, 1971; Volume 11, 1977; Volume 23, 1981; Volume 58, 1990; Volume 69, 1992; Volume 99; 1999.